JUST LATIN

Progressive piano solos

ARRANGED BY STEPHEN DURO

Chester Music
(A division of Music Sales Limited)
8/9 Frith Street
London W1V 5TZ

£7.99

PREFACE

Here are 15 songs carefully chosen from the repertory of Latin 'standards'. Playing these arrangements calls for particular interpretative skills and to help you in your performance here are a few suggestions.

Some of the pieces in this collection show the influence of jazz. Typical of the jazz style of playing is the grouping of quavers. Quaver passages such as ♩♩♩♩ should sometimes be played as if notated ♩♩♩♩ . This does not apply to all the songs and you, as performer, need to exercise discretion in choosing whether or not to 'interpret' phrases in this manner.

The songs are arranged according to difficulty, with the easier pieces (approximately Grade II standard of the Associated Board) appearing first, and the harder ones (Grade V/VI standard) towards the end. Fingering, where indicated, is intended as a guide only and should be altered to suit the needs of individual players.

Stephen Duro

This book © Copyright 1996 Chester Music
Order No. CH61217 ISBN 0-7119-5955-2

Music processed by Stephen Duro.
Cover design by 4i Limited.
Printed in the United Kingdom by Caligraving Limited, Thetford, Norfolk

CONTENTS

AMAPOLA

Words by Albert Gamse, music by Joseph M. Lacalle

Play this melody with warmth. One way of achieving this is by using the sustaining pedal. For example, try using the pedal in bars 5 and 6 and in other places where there are broken chords in the left hand.

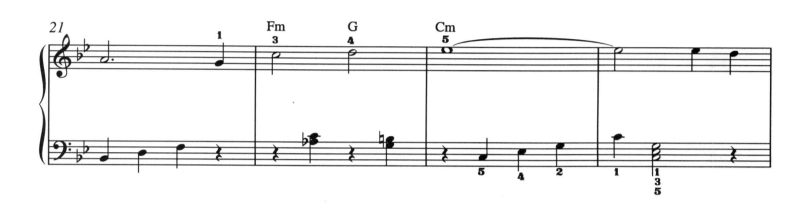

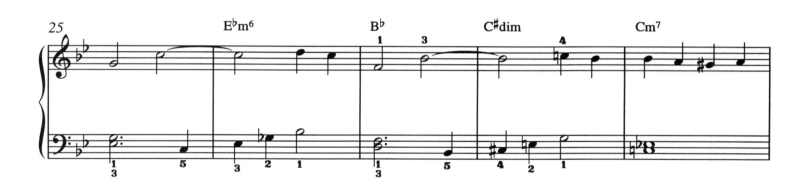

HOW INSENSITIVE

Music by Antonio Carlos Jobim
Original lyrics by Vinicius De Moraes

In this song the melody and harmonic progressions
conjure up an atmosphere reminiscent of Chopin.
When playing it a delicate touch is required.

LA PALOMA

By S. Yradier

This charming beguine, once beloved by Palm Court orchestras, needs to be performed in a reflective style. The rhythmic accompaniment requires a light touch (as in bars 1 and 4 to 6), with just enough intensity to suggest a Mediterranean scene by night.

Moderate beguine

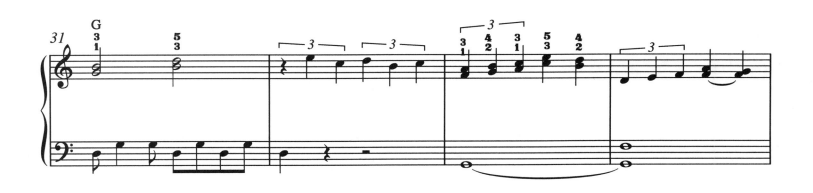

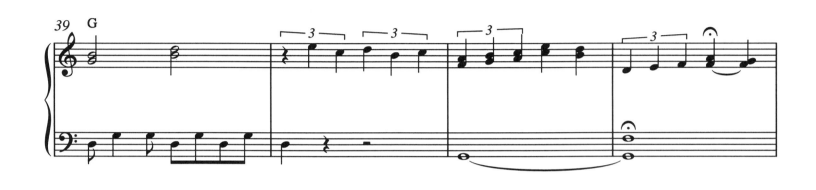

MISIRLOU

Spanish words by J. Pina, music by N. Roubanis

This exotic sounding piece needs to be played in a relaxed, lazy sort of way. The bass ostinato needs to be understated throughout, to evoke the sound of muffled drum beats heard in the distance.

QUIET NIGHTS OF QUIET STARS (CORCOVADO)

Music and original words by Antonio Carlos Jobim

The title of this piece evokes an exquisite nocturnal scene. The accompanying chords should be played in a gentle, insinuating way, reminiscent of the strumming of a quiet guitar.

Moderately

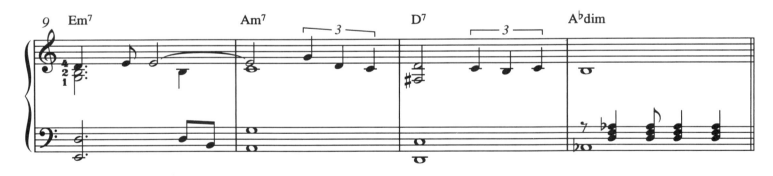

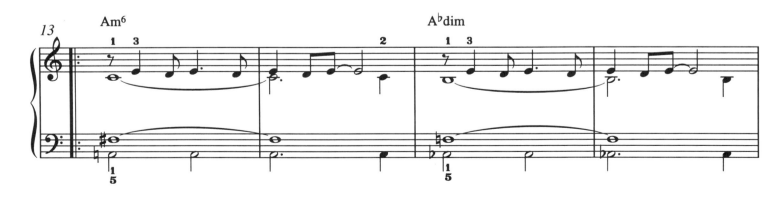

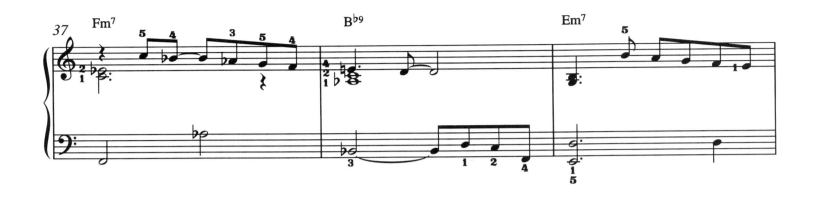

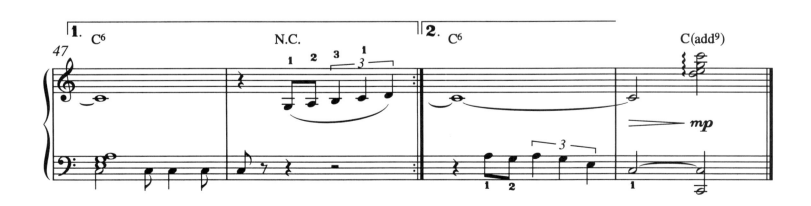

MEDITATION

Original words by Newton Mendonca
Music by Antonio Carlos Jobim

The samba origins of the bossa nova are often discernible, as in this piece by Jobim. Nevertheless, the dance-like bass line should be lightly pointed, and never allowed to sound heavy.

Moderately

THE GIRL FROM IPANEMA

Original words by Vinicius De Moraes
Music by Antonio Carlos Jobim

This song is in an AABA form. The A material consists of a melody which has a characteristic bossa rhythmic feel. The B material consists of longer phrases which build to a climax at bar 31 before returning to the original theme.

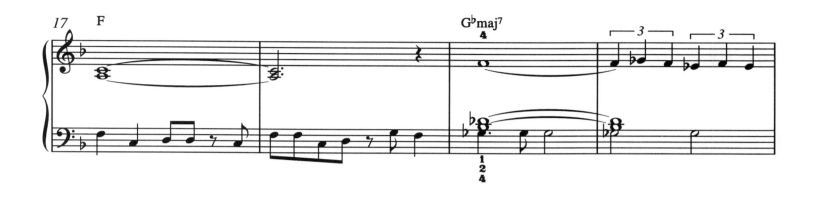

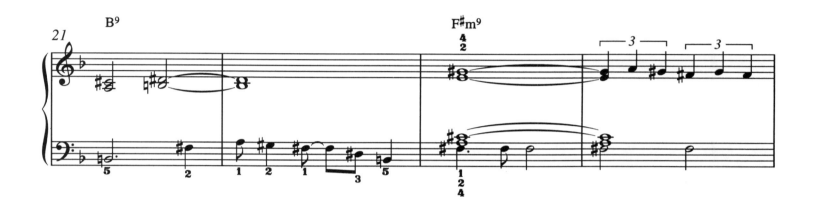

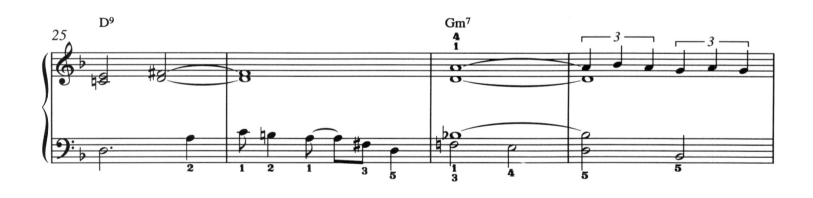

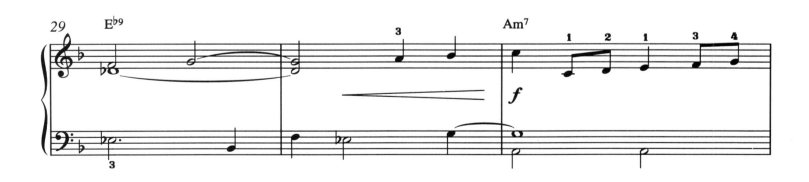

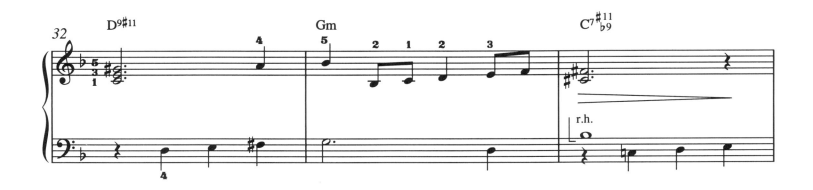

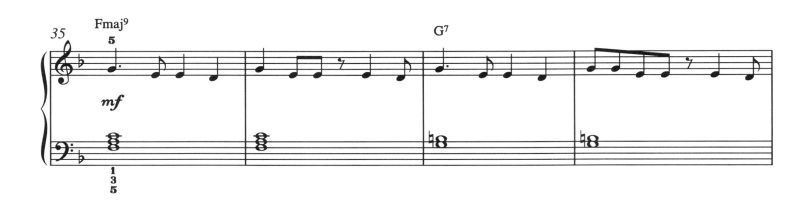

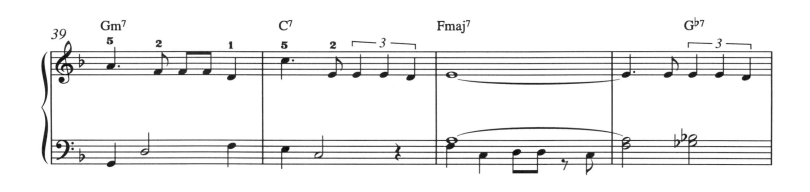

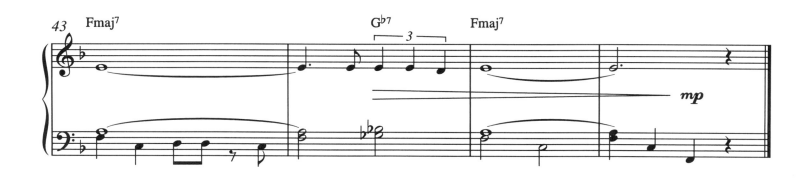

ADIOS

Music and Spanish words by Enric Madriguera

This song features a distinctive counter-melody, first stated in the introduction. When the main theme appears (the pick-up note at the end of bar 4) try to 'bring out' this tune, by playing the counter-melody more softly.

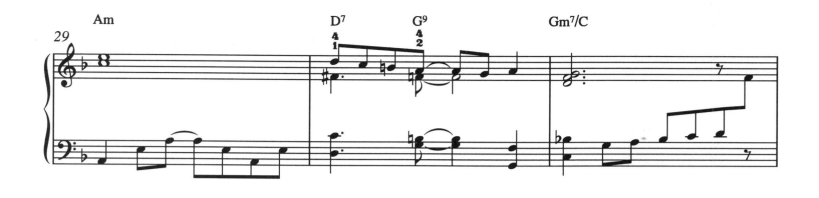

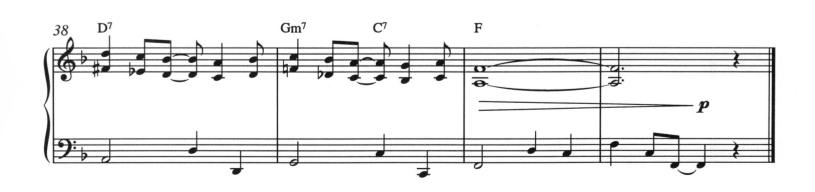

GREEN EYES

Words by L. Wolfe Gilbert and Reg Connelly
Music by Nilo Menendez

A favourite among Latin formation dance teams. As is often the case with Latin tunes, this piece needs to be played with a fairly light touch throughout and with a secure sense of rhythm.

DESAFINADO (SLIGHTLY OUT OF TUNE)

Music by Antonio Carlos Jobim

A very effective piece in terms of melody and form. The main melodic material is contained within the four bars beginning at bar 5. Try to shape this four bar phrase, and its subsequent variations, by lightly accenting the melody note on the first beat of the third bar.

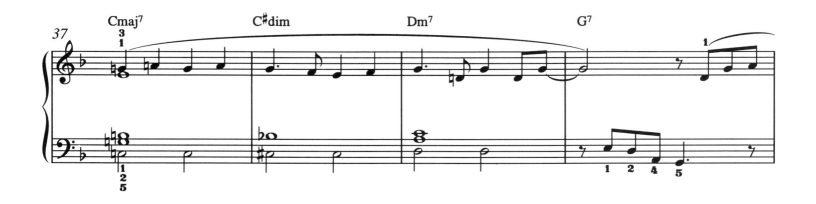

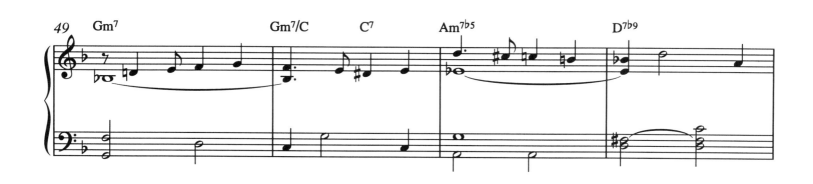

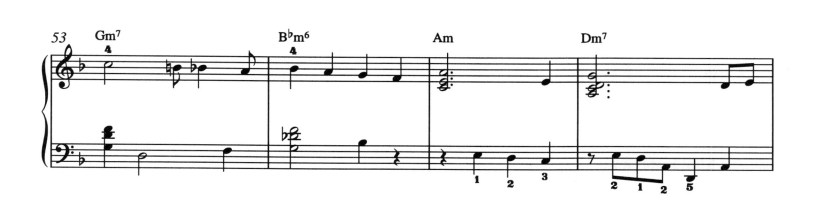

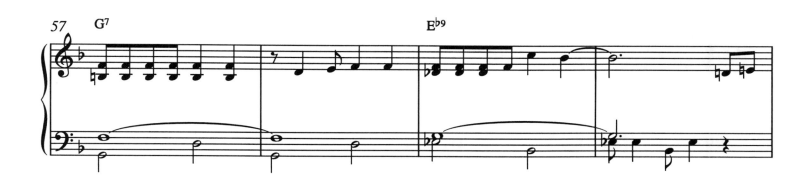

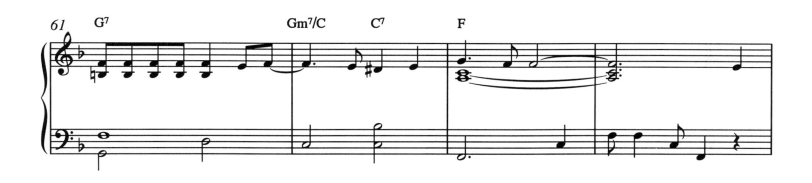

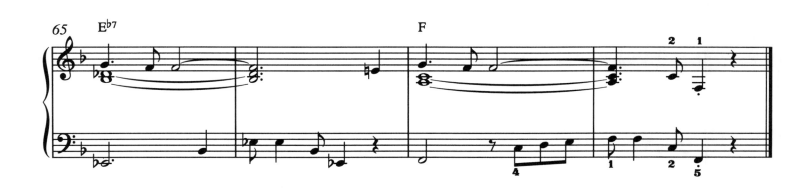

ADIOS MUCHACHOS

Music by Julio Sanders

A typical feature of the ballroom type of tango is the placing of strong accents on the last semiquaver of a bar. There is opportunity to use this effect in the opening two bars, and elsewhere at the discretion of the performer, but it shouldn't be overdone!

SO NICE

Music and original lyrics by Marcos Valle and Paulo Sergio Valle

Typical of the relaxed type of bossa nova, this melody needs to be sensitively shaped throughout. Try to avoid putting too strong an accent on melody notes which are anticipated, as in bar 6.

Relaxed bossa nova

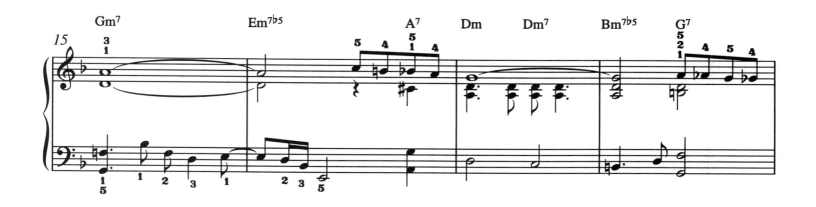

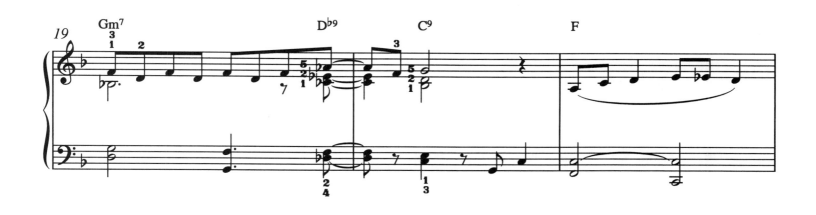

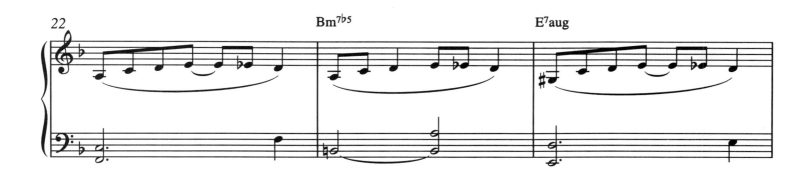

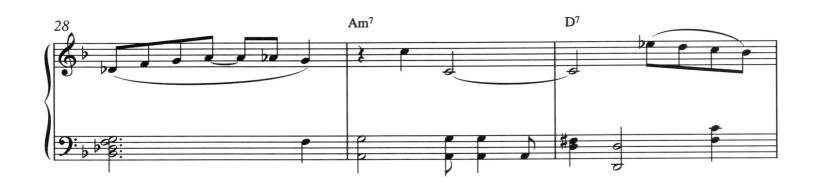

ONE NOTE SAMBA

Original words by N. Mendonca, music by Antonio Carlos Jobim

This piece features a single note melody line: interest is maintained by means of subtle variations in rhythm and harmony. The charm of this music lies in the feeling of understatement, so it is best to avoid strong accents except where special dramatic effect is needed – as in the final bars!

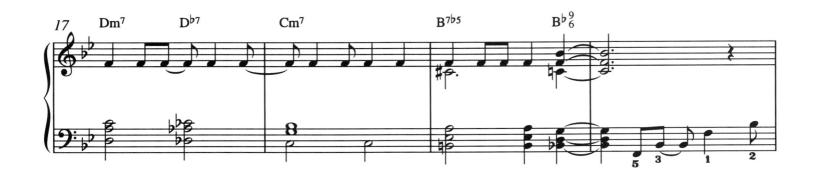

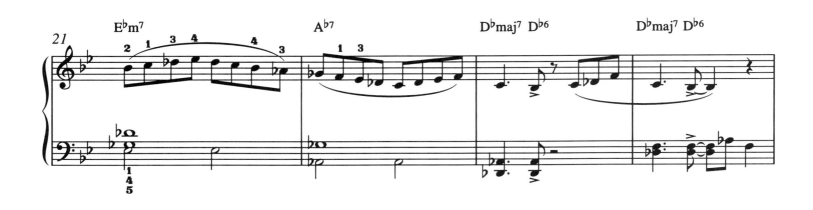

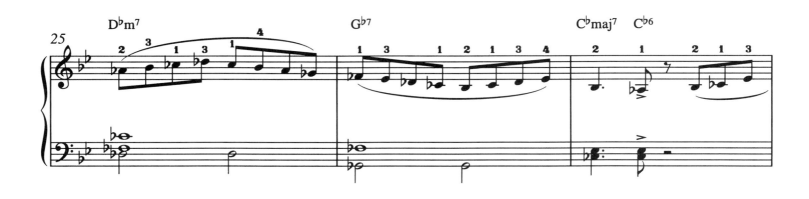

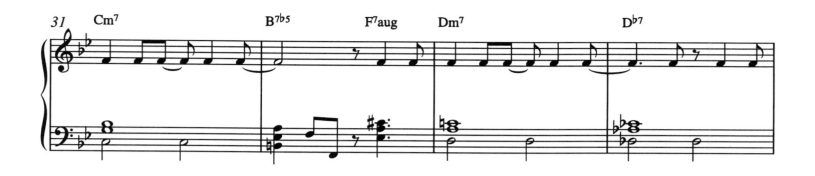

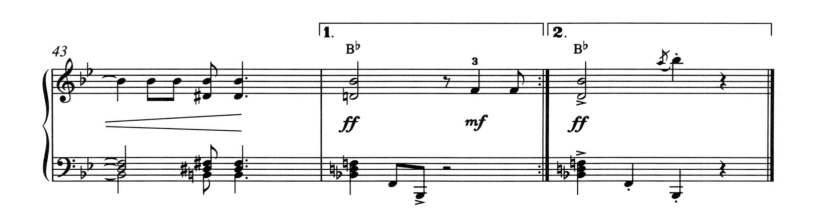

WAVE

Words and music by Antonio Carlos Jobim

The subtlety of this piece arises from the mixture of major and minor tonality, and the rhythmic mix inherent in the piece. For the latter, try to distinguish the subtle difference between the bossa nova style (bars 9-10 in the right hand, for example) from the more jazz inflected rhythms (the left hand figure in bars 11-12).

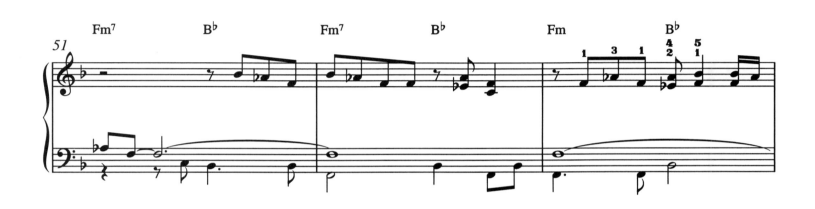

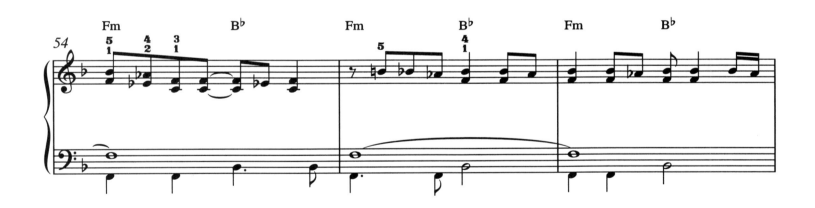

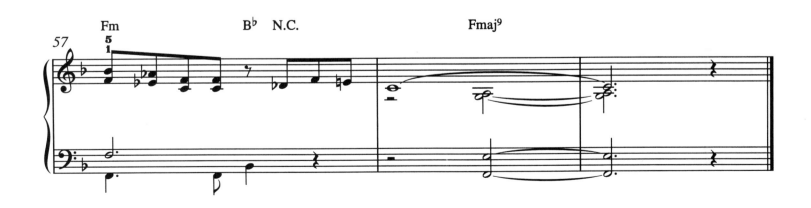

DELICADO

By Waldyr Azevedo

In this composition strong rhythmical writing in both hands alternates with a flowing melody in the right hand. The former calls for a mildly percussive style of playing with little pedal, whereas the melodic passages should be played with warmth.

Tempo di baião